Listen for It

Focus | The letters **b**, **f**, and **r** are consonants. Each consonant has a sound. Words may begin or end with a **b**, an **f**, or an **r**.

b	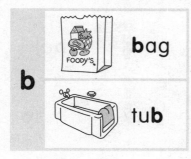 **b**ag		**f**	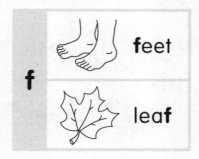 **f**eet	**r**	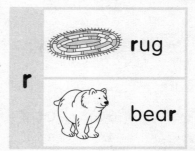 **r**ug
	tu**b**			lea**f**		bea**r**

Say the sound of the letter. Then say the picture name.
Fill in the circle to show if you hear the letter-sound **first** or **last**.

1.
b
○——○

2.
b
○——○

3.
b
○——○

4.
f
○——○

5.
f
○——○

6.
f
○——○

7.
r
○——○

8.
r
○——○

9.
r
○——○

Dictation •

1. ___at   2. ___at   3. ___at   4. fa___   5. bee___   6. ri___

Listen for It

Focus The letters **k**, **m**, and **p** are consonants. Each consonant has a sound. Words may begin or end with a **k**, an **m**, or a **p**.

k — **k**ey / boo**k**

m — **m**en / far**m**

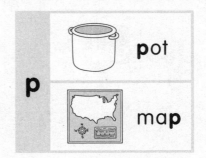

p — **p**ot / ma**p**

Say the sound of the letter. Then say the picture name.
Fill in the circle to show if you hear the letter-sound **first** or **last**.

1.

k

2.

k

3.

k

4.

m

5.

m

6.

m

7.

p

8.

p

9.

p

Dictation ....

1. ___it   2. ___itt   3. ___it   4. loo___   5. kee___   6. mo___

Write It

Letter Box

b   f   k   m   p   r

Say the picture name.
Then write the letter that stands for the **first** or **last** sound you hear.

1.  ma___	2. ___us	3. roo___	4. ___at
5. ___ing	6. tu___	7. ___en	8. ___eet
9.  mas___	10. ca___	11. gu___	12. ___en

Dictation ....

1. ___i___   2. ___o___   3. ___i___   4. ___oo___

Listen for It

Focus The letters **d**, **l**, and **n** are consonants. Each consonant has a sound. Words may begin or end with a **d**, an **l**, or an **n**.

d — **d**ime, mu**d**

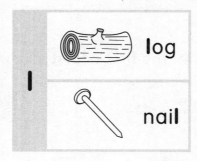

l — **l**og, nai**l**

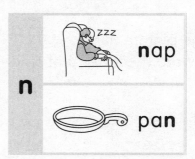

n — **n**ap, pa**n**

Say the sound of the letter. Then say the picture name.
Fill in the circle to show if you hear the letter-sound **first** or **last**.

1. **d** ○——○	2. **d** ○——○	3. **d** ○——○
4. **l** ○——○	5. **l** ○——○	6. **l** ○——○
7. **n** ○——○	8. **n** ○——○	9. **n** ○——○

Dictation ···

1. ___ot   2. ___ot   3. ___ot   4. pa___   5. lio___   6. nee___

Write It

Letter Box

d l n

Say the picture name.
Then write the letter that stands for the **first** or **last** sound you hear.

1.  mu ___	2. ___ ose	3. ___ eaf	4. ___ eer
5. pai ___	6. ma ___	7. ___ amp	8. be ___
9. ___ eck	10. ___ ime	11. pa ___	12. mai ___

Dictation

1. ___ i ___   2. ___ o ___   3. ___ e ___   4. ___ ai ___

Listen for It

Focus The letters **s**, **t**, and **v** are consonants. Each consonant has a sound.

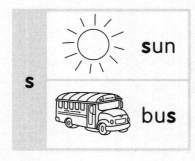
s — sun / bus

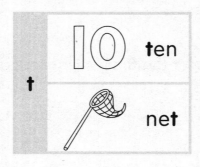
t — ten / net

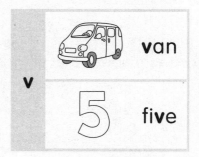
v — van / five

Say the sound of the letter. Then say the picture name.
Fill in the circle to show if you hear the letter-sound **first** or **last**.

1.
s
○──○

2.
s
○──○

3.
s
○──○

4.
t
○──○

5.
t
○──○

6.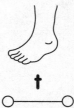
t
○──○

7.
v
○──○

8.
v
○──○

9.
v
○──○

Dictation ••

1. ___op   2. ___et   3. ___et   4. ves___   5. sa___e   6. thi___

  Daily Phonics • EMC 6773 • © Evan-Moor Corp.

Listen for It

Focus The letters **h** and **w** are consonants. Each consonant has a sound. You can usually hear **h** and **w** when they are at the beginning of words, but not when they are at the end.

h  **h**am   **w**  **w**eb

Say the picture name.
Then circle the letter that stands for the **first** sound you hear.

1.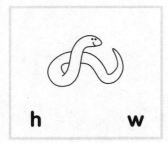
   h   w

2.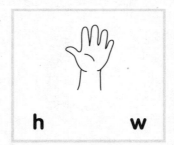
   h   w

3.
   h   w

4.
   h   w

5.
   h   w

6.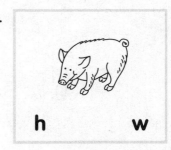
   h   w

7.
   h   w

8.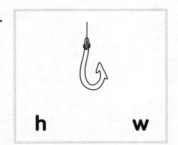
   h   w

9.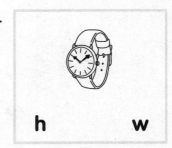
   h   w

Dictation ••

1. ___ood   2. ___im   3. ___ood   4. ___in

Listen for It

Focus The letters **j** and **y** are consonants. When **j** is the first letter in a word, it usually has the sound you hear at the beginning of **jet**. When **y** is the first letter in a word, it usually has the sound you hear at the beginning of **yarn**.

j  jet   **y**  yarn

Say the picture name.
Then circle the letter that stands for the **first** sound you hear.

1.
j   y

2.
j   y

3.
j   y

4.
j   y

5.
j   y

6.
j   y

7.
j   y

8.
j   y

9.
j   y

Dictation •

1. ___ob   2. ___et   3. ___ust   4. ___es

Listen for It

Focus The letters **q**, **x**, and **z** are consonants. The letters **q** and **u** appear together in many words. The letter **x** is often at the end of a word. Not many words begin or end with the letter **z**.

 **q** **q**ueen    **x** fo**x**    **z** **z**ero

Say the sound that the bold letter stands for. Then say the picture name. For rows 1 and 3, fill in the circle if the picture name **begins** with that sound. For row 2, fill in the circle if the picture name **ends** with that sound.

Dictation

1. ___ip   2. ___uit   3. ___ebra   4. fi___   5. wa___

Write It

Letter Box

| h | j | s | t | v | w | x | y |

Say the picture name.
Then write the letter that stands for the **first** or **last** letter-sound you hear.

1.  ve ___	2. si ___	3. ___ et	4. ___ et
5. ___ ood	6.  wa ___ e	7. ___ and	8. ___ en
9. ___ am	10. ___ est	11. nut ___	12. ___ ak

Dictation

1. I am in the ___ o ___ ___ u ___.   2. The ___ a ___ is ___ e ___.

Listen for It

> **Focus**
> The letters **a** and **e** are vowels. Vowels can have a **short** sound.
> You hear the **short a** sound in **hand**.
> You hear the **short e** sound in **bed**.

short **a**		short **e**	
h**a**nd		b**e**d	

Say the picture name. Listen for the **short** vowel sound.
Then fill in the circle next to the letter that stands for that sound.

1. ○ **a** ○ **e**	2.  ○ **a** ○ **e**	3. ○ **a** ○ **e**
4. ○ **a** ○ **e**	5. ○ **a** ○ **e**	6. ○ **a** ○ **e**
7. ○ **a** ○ **e**	8. ○ **a** ○ **e**	9. ○ **a** ○ **e**
10. ○ **a** ○ **e**	11. ○ **a** ○ **e**	12. ○ **a** ○ **e**

Dictation •

1. r___n   2. p___n   3. b___d   4. p___t   5. s___d

Write It

Letter Box

a   e

Say the picture name. Write the letter that stands for the **short** vowel sound you hear. Then read the word.

1.	2.	3.	4.
			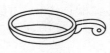
j___t	c___b	b___d	p___n

5.	6.	7.	8.
r___t	p___n	m___p	y___k

9.	10.	11.	12.
m___n	w___b	n___p	c___p

Dictation

1. ___ ___ ___   2. ___ ___ ___   3. ___ ___ ___   4. ___ ___ ___

Listen for It

Focus
The letters **i**, **o**, and **u** are vowels. Vowels can have a **short** sound.
You hear the **short i** sound in **six**.
You hear the **short o** sound in **dot**.
You hear the **short u** sound in **tub**.

| short **i** **six** | 6 | short **o** **dot** | ● | short **u** **tub** | |

Say the picture name. Listen for the **short** vowel sound.
Then circle the vowel that stands for that sound.

1.
   i   o   u

2.
   i   o   u

3.
   i   o   u

4.
   i   o   u

5.
   i   o   u

6.
   i   o   u

7.
   i   o   u

8.
   i   o   u

9.
   i   o   u

10.
    i   o   u

11.
    i   o   u

12.
    i   o   u

Dictation ....

1. d__p   2. b__x   3. r__n   4. p__p   5. r__p

Write It

Letter Box

i   o   u

Say the picture name. Write the letter that stands for the **short** vowel sound you hear. Then read the word.

1.  m ___ p	2. c ___ p	3. f ___ x	4. 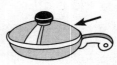 l ___ d
5. n ___ t	6. s ___ x	7. l ___ ck	8.  h ___ ll
9.  j ___ mp	10. p ___ t	11.  c ___ t	12. d ___ g

Dictation

1. ___ ___ ___   2. ___ ___ ___   3. ___ ___ ___   4. ___ ___ ___

Read It

Write the missing words. Then read the sentence.

1.

   lid   pan

   The _____ is on the _____.

2.

   hen   pet   Jim

   _____ has a _____ _____.

3.

   dug   nut   Sam

   _____ _____ up a _____.

4.

   can   box   top

   Put the _____ on _____ of the _____.

Dictation ....

_____ will _____ and take a _____.

Listen for It

Focus   A vowel between two consonants has a **short** sound.

 van  hen  pig  cot  nut

Say the picture name. Listen for the **short** vowel sound.
Then write the letter that stands for that sound.

1. f___n	2.  h___t	3. 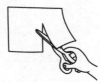 c___t
4. t___n	5. w___g	6. m___p
7. s___d	8. w___b	9. h___g

Dictation ....

1. _____ 2. _____ 3. _____ 4. _____ 5. _____

Listen for It

Focus — Words that have a vowel between two consonants are called **CVC** words. The vowel in a CVC word has a **short** sound.

 rat    jet    pin    fox    sun

Say the picture name. Listen for the **short** vowel sound.
Then fill in the circle next to the word that has that vowel sound.

1.  ○ pan ○ pen	2. ○ bad ○ bed	3. ○ zap ○ zip
4. ○ mop ○ map	5. ○ net ○ nut	6. ○ man ○ men
7. ○ fan ○ fin	8.  ○ cub ○ cab	9. ○ top ○ tip

Dictation ....

1. _____   2. _____   3. _____   4. _____   5. _____

Write It

Word Box

mat	fox	hen
bus	rip	cup
jam	net	pin

Say the picture name. Then write the word on the line.

1.
_____

2.
_____

3.
_____

4.
_____

5.
_____

6.
_____

7.
_____

8.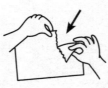
_____

9.
_____

Dictation

1. _____ _____   2. _____ _____   3. _____ _____

Write It

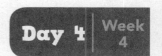

Say the picture name. Read the words.
Circle the word that names the picture. Then write the word on the line.

#					
1.		cap	cup	cop	_____
2.		not	nut	net	_____
3.		fan	fun	fin	_____
4.		pet	put	pot	_____
5.		tin	ten	tan	_____
6.		pup	pep	pop	_____

Dictation ....

Dad _____ red _____ on his _____.

Read It

Write the missing words. Then read the sentence.

1.

   bag   can

   Put the _____ in the _____.

2.

   map   rip

   Do not _____ the _____.

3.

   wet   mop

   The _____ is _____.

4.

   bus   dog   let

   Tim _____ the _____ onto the _____.

5.

   red   cap   sun

   My _____ has a _____ _____ on it.

Dictation ....

My _____ _____ _____ _____.

Listen for It

Focus A vowel can have a **long** sound. The long sound says the vowel's name. You hear the **long a** sound in **vase**. You hear the **long e** sound in **me**.

long **a**		long **e**	
v**a**se		m**e**	

Say the picture name. Listen to the **long** vowel sound.
Then circle the vowel that stands for that sound.

1.	2.	3.
a e	a e	 a e

1.
 a   e
2. a   e
3. a   e

4.  a   e
5.  a   e
6. a   e

7. a   e
8. a   e
9. a   e

Dictation ....

1. w____   2. ____pe   3. h____   4. s____me

Listen for It

Focus A vowel can have a **long** sound. The long sound says the vowel's name. You hear the **long i** sound in **nine**. You hear the **long o** sound in **bone**. You hear the **long u** sound in **cube**.

| long **i** nine | | long **o** bone | | long **u** cube | |

Say the picture name. Listen to the **long** vowel sound.
Then circle the letter that stands for that sound.

1.

i   o   u

2.

i   o   u

3.

i   o   u

4.

i   o   u

5.

i   o   u

6.

i   o   u

7.

i   o   u

8.

i   o   u

9.

i   o   u

Dictation •••

1. n___te   2. t___ne   3. h___ke   4. r___be

Write It

Letter Box

a   e   i   o   u

Say the picture name.
Then write the letter that stands for the **long** vowel sound you hear.

1.  h ___ me	2.  c ___ ve	3.  c ___ te
4. m ___	5. f ___ ve	6. c ___ ke
7. t ___ re	8. b ___ ne	9. m ___ le

Dictation •

1. l ___ te   2. k ___ te   3. w ___   4. n ___ te   5. ___ se

Write It

Letter Box

a   e   i   o   u

Say the picture name. Listen to the **long** vowel sound.
Then write the letter that stands for that sound.

1. _____ l ___ ne	2. r ___ ke	3. m ___ le
4. m ___ le	5. p ___ le	6. p ___ le
7.  w ___ de	8. w ___ ed	9.  w ___ de

Dictation ••

1. b ___ ke   2. h ___ me   3. t ___ be   4. s ___ me   5. w ___ ek

Review It

Say the picture name.
Circle the picture when you hear a **long** vowel sound.
Underline the picture when you hear a **short** vowel sound.

1.	**a**				
2.	**e**				
3.	**i**				
4.	**o**				
5.	**u**				

Dictation ....

1. W___ve to the m___le.   2. H___de the b___ne.

Read It

Focus Some words have a CVCe pattern. The vowel in the middle has a **long** sound. The **e** at the end is silent.

 kit + **e** = kite

Read the word. Add a final **e** to make a new word.
Then fill in the circle under the picture that matches the new word.

1.

tub___

○   ○

2.

man___

○   ○

3.

rob___

○   ○

4.

tap___

○   ○

5.

pin___

○   ○

6.

pan___

○   ○

Dictation ···

1. _____ _____   2. _____ _____

Read It

Focus   The vowel in the middle of a CVCe word has a **long** sound. The final **e** is silent.

Letter Box

a	e	i	o	u

Say the picture name.
Write the letter that stands for the **long** vowel sound.
Then write the silent **e** at the end of the word.

1. t___p___	2. k___t___	3. b___k___
4. r___p___	5. p___p___	6. n___m___
7. t___b___	8. fr___m___	9.  sm___k___

Dictation •

1. t___m___   2. r___d___   3. n___t___   4. t___n___

Write It

Word Box

hid	hide	hole	pine
rake	mule	pin	rope

Say the picture name. Then write the word on the lines.
You will use only six of the words in the box.

1. ___ ___ ___ ___

2. ___ ___ ___ ___

3. ___ ___ ___

4. ___ ___ ___ ___

5. ___ ___ ___

6. ___ ___ ___ ___

Dictation

1. _____   2. _____   3. _____   4. _____

Write It

Say the picture name. Read the words.
Circle the word that names the picture. Then write the word on the line.

1.	rope	ripe	_____
2.	bake	bike	_____
3.	dome	dime	_____
4.	tune	tube	_____
5.	pole	pile	_____
6.	lone	lane	_____
7.	mile	mole	_____
8.	mane	mine	_____

Dictation

1. _____   2. _____   3. _____   4. _____

Read It

Write the missing words. Then read the sentence.

1.

   cone   pine

   A _____ _____ has seeds.

2.

   mole   hole

   A _____ can dig a _____.

3.

   name   same

   Mom and I have the _____ _____.

4.

   bikes   rule

   What is the _____ about _____?

5.

   mule   ride   safe

   It is _____ to _____ that _____.

Dictation

Tom will _____ the _____.

Listen for It

Focus A syllable is a word part that has one vowel sound. A word can have more than one syllable.

gate
1 vowel sound = **1** syllable

napkin
2 vowel sounds = **2** syllables

Say each picture name. Listen for the vowel sounds. Write how many vowel sounds you hear. Then write how many syllables the word has.

		vowel sounds	syllables
1.			
2.			
3.			
4.			
5.			
6.			

Dictation ···

1. _____ ☐   2. _____ ☐   3. _____ ☐

Listen for It

Focus Many words have two syllables. The first syllable ends with a consonant. The second syllable begins with a consonant. Both syllables have a vowel sound.

mag·net

ten·nis

Say the picture name.
Then draw a line to divide the word into syllables.

1. rabbit	2. button	3. napkin
4. basket	5. muffin	6. sunset
7. puppet	8. letter	9. pretzel

Dictation ••

1. _____ ☐   2. _____ ☐   3. _____ ☐

Read It

Focus A syllable that ends in a consonant is called a **closed** syllable. The vowels in a closed syllable usually have a **short** sound.

muf•fin

Look at the syllables in the word. Underline the vowel or vowels that have a **short** sound. Then blend the syllables to read the word.

1. pump•kin	2. pen•ny	3. ro•bot
4. ho•tel	5. pup•py	6. men•u
7. up•set	8. nap•kin	9. lim•it

Dictation ....

1. _____   2. _____

Read It

Focus | A syllable that ends in a vowel is called an **open** syllable. The first vowel in an open syllable usually has a **long** sound.

ro•bot

Look at the syllables in the word. Underline the vowel that has a **long** sound. Then read the word out loud.

1. hu•man	2. tu•lip	3. ba•by
4. $\begin{array}{r} 4 \\ -2 \\ \hline 2 \end{array}$ mi•nus	5. la•dy	6. pi•lot
7. yo•yo	8. mu•sic	9. o•pen

Dictation ••

1. _____   2. _____

Read It

Look at the syllable that is underlined in each word. Read the word out loud. Then check the correct boxes. The first one has been done for you.

	closed syllable	open syllable	short vowel	long vowel
1. <u>ba</u>con		✓		✓
2. <u>rot</u>ten				
3. <u>pen</u>ny				
4. rab<u>bit</u>				
5. hell<u>o</u>				
6. <u>pu</u>pil				
7. ro<u>bot</u>				
8. <u>ze</u>bra				

Dictation ••

Listen for It

Focus When a word ends with a consonant + **y**, the **y** has a vowel sound. The **y** has a **long i** or **long e** sound.

| y = long **i** sky |  | y = long **e** penny | |

Say the picture name. Then read the word. Listen to the sound of **y**.
Circle **long i** or **long e** to show which long vowel sound you hear.

1.
cry
long i   **long e**

2.
puppy
long i   **long e**

3.
lady
long i   **long e**

4.
spy
long i   **long e**

5.
fry
long i   **long e**

6.
baby
long i   **long e**

7.
pony
long i   **long e**

8.
fly
long i   **long e**

9.
bunny
long i   **long e**

Dictation ••

1. _____   2. _____   3. _____

Listen for It

Focus A **y** usually has the **long i** sound in words that have one syllable.
A **y** usually has the **long e** sound in words that have two syllables.

sky long **i**	☁☀︎	**1** syllable	penny long **e**	🪙	**2** syllables

Say the word. How many syllables do you hear?
Fill in the circle next to that number.
Then fill in the circle next to **i** or **e** to show what sound the **y** has.

1. sunny

syllables	sound
○ **1**	○ **i**
○ **2**	○ **e**

2. bunny

syllables	sound
○ **1**	○ **i**
○ **2**	○ **e**

3. spy

syllables	sound
○ **1**	○ **i**
○ **2**	○ **e**

4. pony

syllables	sound
○ **1**	○ **i**
○ **2**	○ **e**

5. cry

syllables	sound
○ **1**	○ **i**
○ **2**	○ **e**

6. fry

syllables	sound
○ **1**	○ **i**
○ **2**	○ **e**

Dictation ··

1. _____   2. _____   3. _____

Write It

Word Box

fly	happy	my	funny	fry
sky	pony	baby	cry	puppy

Read the word. Do you hear **long i** or **long e**?
Write the word in the correct box.

y = long **i**	**y** = long **e**
_____	_____
_____	_____
_____	_____
_____	_____
_____	_____

Dictation ••

1. _____   2. _____   3. _____

Review It

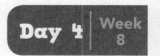

Say the picture name. Then read the words.
Circle the word that names the picture.

1.		sixty	sky	spy
2.		lady	baby	daddy
3.		sly	try	fry
4.		puppy	pony	penny
5.		sunny	funny	silly
6.		try	fry	fly
7.		penny	puppy	pony
8.		spy	sly	sky

Dictation ···

_____

_____

Read It

Write the missing words. Then read the sentence.

1.

    baby happy

    The cute _____ is _____.

2.

    spy funny

    Is that _____ man a _____?

3.

    pony try

    I will _____ to ride a _____.

4.

    fly sky

    The kite will _____ in the _____.

5.

    puppy lady my

    Did the _____ see _____ _____?

Dictation ••

_____

Listen for It

Focus The letter **c** can have the **hard** sound of **/k/** or the **soft** sound of **/s/**. The letter **c** usually has the **/k/** sound when it is followed by an **a**, an **o**, or a **u**.

c = /k/ sound

 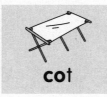 

cat   **co**t   **cu**p

Look at the word. Does the **c** have the **/k/** sound?
Fill in the circle next to **yes** or **no**.

1.  cake	2. can	3.  ice
○ yes ○ no	○ yes ○ no	○ yes ○ no
4.  corn	5. face	6. cube
○ yes ○ no	○ yes ○ no	○ yes ○ no

Dictation ....

1. _____   2. _____   3. _____

Listen for It

Focus   The letter **c** can have the **hard** sound of **/k/** or the **soft** sound of **/s/**. The letter **c** usually has the **/s/** sound when it is followed by an **e** or an **i**.

c = /s/ sound

fac**e**

ci**ty**

Look at the word. Does the **c** have the **/s/** sound?
Fill in the circle next to **yes** or **no**.

1. cent ○ yes ○ no	2. cane ○ yes ○ no	3. rice ○ yes ○ no
4. cub ○ yes ○ no	5. fence ○ yes ○ no	6. pencil ○ yes ○ no

Dictation ···

1. _____   2. _____   3. _____

Listen for It

Focus The letter **g** can have the **hard** sound of **/g/** or the **soft** sound of **/j/**. The letter **g** usually has the **/g/** sound when it is followed by an **a**, an **o**, or a **u**, or when it is the last letter of a word.

g = /g/ sound

 gas

 gold

 gum

 fro**g**

Look at the word. Does the **g** have the **/g/** sound?
Fill in the circle next to **yes** or **no**.

1.

gem

○ yes   ○ no

2.

bug

○ yes   ○ no

3.

orange

○ yes   ○ no

4.

gate

○ yes   ○ no

5.

wagon

○ yes   ○ no

6.

gull

○ yes   ○ no

Dictation ....

1. _____   2. _____   3. _____   4. _____

Listen for It

Focus The letter **g** can have the **hard** sound of /g/ or the **soft** sound of /j/. The letter **g** usually has the /j/ sound when it is followed by an **e** or an **i**.

g = /j/ sound

gem

giant

Look at the word. Does the **g** have the /j/ sound?
Fill in the circle next to **yes** or **no**.

1. gum ○ yes ○ no	2. cage ○ yes ○ no	3.  golf ○ yes ○ no
4.  page ○ yes ○ no	5.  magic ○ yes ○ no	6.  gas ○ yes ○ no

Dictation •

1. ___el   2. a___e

Read It

Say the picture name. Write a **c** or a **g** to spell the word.
Then write the words to complete the sentence. Read the sentence out loud.

1. ___um   ___ent

The _____ costs one _____.

---

2.  wa___on   fla___

Put the _____ in the _____.

---

3.  ___age   mi___e

The _____ ran inside a large _____.

---

4.  ___ave   ___iant

Does a _____ sleep in this _____?

---

5.  hu___e   ___ate

The mice cannot open the _____ _____.

Dictation ....

I have _____ on my _____!

Listen for It

Focus Two consonant sounds said together are called a **consonant blend**. Many words begin with a **consonant + l** blend.

cl	**fl**	**gl**	**pl**
club	**fl**ip	**gl**ad	**pl**ot

Say the picture name.
Then fill in the circle next to the blend you hear at the **beginning**.

1.
   - ○ cl
   - ○ fl
   - ○ pl

2.
   - ○ cl
   - ○ fl
   - ○ pl

3.
   - ○ gl
   - ○ pl
   - ○ fl

4.
   - ○ cl
   - ○ fl
   - ○ pl

5.
   - ○ cl
   - ○ fl
   - ○ pl

6.
   - ○ gl
   - ○ pl
   - ○ fl

7.
   - ○ cl
   - ○ fl
   - ○ pl

8.
   - ○ gl
   - ○ pl
   - ○ fl

9.
   - ○ cl
   - ○ fl
   - ○ pl

Dictation ....

1. _____ 2. _____ 3. _____

Listen for It

Focus   Two consonant sounds said together are called a **consonant blend**. Many words begin with a **consonant + r** blend.

br	**dr**	**gr**	**tr**
brave	**dr**ill	**gr**in	**tr**ade

Say the picture name.
Then fill in the circle next to the blend you hear at the **beginning**.

1.  ○ br ○ dr ○ tr	2. 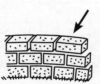 ○ br ○ dr ○ tr	3. ○ br ○ gr ○ tr
4. ○ br ○ gr ○ tr	5. ○ br ○ dr ○ tr	6. ○ br ○ dr ○ tr
7.  ○ br ○ dr ○ tr	8. ○ br ○ dr ○ tr	9. ○ br ○ dr ○ tr

Dictation ....

1. _____   2. _____   3. _____

Write It and Read It

Letter Box

cl	fl	gl	pl	br	dr	gr	tr

Say the picture name.
Then write the blend to spell the word.

1.

___ ___ee

2.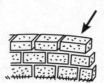

___ ___ick

3.

___ ___apes

4.

___ ___obe

5.

___ ___ug

6.

___ ___ame

Write the words that complete the sentence.
Then read the sentence.

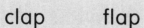

1. clap   flap   flip

Will you _____ when I do a _____?

2. drum   grin   grip

Fran will _____ when she sees her new _____.

Dictation

....

_____

Listen for It

Focus Some consonant blends begin with the letter **s**. These blends can have one or two consonants after the **s**.

sk	sl	sp	sw	spl	str
skip	**sl**am	**sp**ell	**sw**im	**spl**it	**str**ipe

Say the picture name.
Then fill in the circle next to the blend you hear at the **beginning**.

1.
○ sk
○ sl
○ sp

2.
○ sw
○ spl
○ str

3.
○ sk
○ sl
○ sp

4.
○ sk
○ sl
○ sp

5.
○ sw
○ spl
○ str

6.
○ spl
○ sl
○ sp

7.
○ sk
○ sl
○ sp

8.
○ sw
○ spl
○ str

9.
○ sw
○ spl
○ str

Dictation ••

1. _____ 2. _____ 3. _____ 4. _____

Write It and Read It

Letter Box

| sk | sl | sp | sw | spl | str |

Say the picture name.
Then write the blend to spell the word.

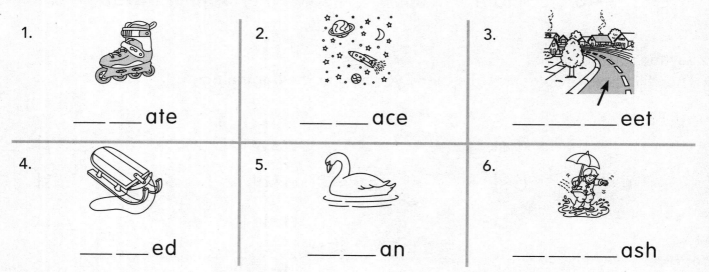

1. ___ ___ ate

2. ___ ___ ace

3. ___ ___ ___ eet

4. ___ ___ ed

5. ___ ___ an

6. ___ ___ ___ ash

Write the words that complete the sentence.
Then read the sentence.

1. slim   splash   swim

Stella can _____ and _____.

2. stripe   split   skunk

A _____ has a wide _____ on its back.

Dictation ....

_____

Listen for It

Focus   A consonant blend may be at the end of a word.
Many words end with a **consonant + t** blend.

ft	**lt**	**nt**	**st**
so**ft**	fe**lt**	mi**nt**	mi**st**

Say the picture name.
Then fill in the circle next to the blend you hear at the **end** of the word.

1.
   ○ ft
   ○ lt
   ○ st

2.
   ○ ft
   ○ lt
   ○ st

3.
   ○ ft
   ○ lt
   ○ nt

4.
   ○ ft
   ○ nt
   ○ st

5.
   ○ ft
   ○ lt
   ○ nt

6.
   ○ ft
   ○ lt
   ○ nt

7.
   ○ ft
   ○ lt
   ○ st

8.
   ○ ft
   ○ nt
   ○ st

9.
   ○ ft
   ○ nt
   ○ st

Dictation ••

1. _____ 2. _____ 3. _____ 4. _____

Write It

Letter Box

| ft | lt | nt | st |

Say the picture name. Write the blend to spell the word.
Then read the word.

1.

ne __ __

2.

gi __ __

3.

te __ __

4.

be __ __

5.

ra __ __

6.

me __ __

7.

cru __ __

8.

ce __ __

9.

ca __ __

Dictation

....

_____

Listen for It

Focus A consonant blend may be at the end of a word. Many words end with the consonant blends **ld**, **nd**, **mp**, or **nk**.

ld	nd	mp	nk
ho**ld**	be**nd**	pu**mp**	pi**nk**

Say the picture name.
Then fill in the circle next to the blend you hear at the **end** of the word.

1. ○ ld ○ mp ○ nd

2. ○ ld ○ mp ○ nk

3. ○ ld ○ mp ○ nd

4. ○ ld ○ nd ○ mp

5. ○ ld ○ mp ○ nk

6. ○ ld ○ nd ○ nk

7. ○ ld ○ nd ○ mp

8. ○ ld ○ nk ○ nd

9. ○ ld ○ nk ○ nd

Dictation

1. _____ 2. _____ 3. _____ 4. _____

Write It

Letter Box

ld	nd	mp	nk

Say the picture name. Write the blend to spell the word.
Then read the word.

1.

ha ___ ___

2.

sku ___ ___

3.

la ___ ___

4.

co ___ ___

5.

sta ___ ___

6.

chi ___ ___

7.

chi ___ ___

8.

wi ___ ___

9.

sa ___ ___

Dictation

_____

Read It

Write the words that complete the sentence.
Then read the sentence out loud.

1.

   link   Gramps   wink

   _____ likes to _____ at me.

2.

   gold   hold   host

   The chest can _____ a lot of _____.

3.

   hand   bunk   bump

   How did you get a _____ on your _____?

4.

   lift   tent   blimp

   The _____ will fly over the _____.

5.

   send   spent   band

   We _____ time with the _____.

Dictation ....

_____

Listen for It

Focus A digraph is two letters together that have one new sound. Many words begin with a **consonant + h** digraph.

ch	sh	th	wh
chip	**sh**ut	**th**in	**wh**en

Say the sound of the two letters. Then say each picture name.
Fill in the circle if the picture name **begins** with that sound.

1. ch-

2. sh-

3. th-

4. wh-

Dictation ....

1. ____ine   2. ____ing   3. ____ose   4. ____ile

Write It

Letter Box

ch   sh   th   wh

Say the picture name. Listen to the **first** sound.
Then write the missing letters to spell the word.

1. _____ _____irt

2. _____ _____ale

3. _____ _____erry

4. _____ _____ain

5. _____ _____ell

6. _____ _____ree

7. _____ _____ave

8. _____ _____est

9. _____ _____eel

10. _____ _____eat

11. _____ _____under

12. _____ _____rimp

Dictation

1. _____   2. _____   3. _____   4. _____

Listen for It

Focus   A digraph may begin or end a word. Many words end with the digraph **ch**, **sh**, or **th**.

ch	sh	th
ri**ch**	ra**sh**	bo**th**

Say the sound of the two letters. Then say each picture name.
Fill in the circle if the picture name **ends** with that sound.

1. -ch

 ○   ○   ○   ○

2. -sh

 ○   ○   ○   ○

3. -th

 ○   ○   ○   ○

Dictation ●●●

1. ca_____   2. su_____   3. clo_____

Write It

Letter Box

ch   sh   th

Say the picture name. Listen to the **last sound**.
Then write the missing letters to spell the word.

1.

wa____ ____

2.

pea____ ____

3.

ba____ ____

4.

ben____ ____

5.

too____ ____

6.

tra____ ____

7.

sandwi____ ____

8.

mo____ ____

9.

fi____ ____

10.

pa____ ____

11.

bu____ ____

12.

in____ ____

Dictation

1. _____

2. _____

3. _____

Read It

Write the words that complete the sentence.
Then read the sentence out loud.

1. both   wash

    We _____ have to _____ the dog.

2. bush   moth

    A white _____ landed on the _____.

3. ranch   sheep

    A flock of _____ live on that _____.

4. chimp   think

    I _____ I see a _____.

5. teeth   whale

    Does a _____ have _____?

Dictation ••

_____

Listen for It

Focus   A digraph is two letters together that have one sound.
The digraphs **ph** and **gh** usually have the /f/ sound.

ph		**ph**one	

gh		lau**gh**	

Say the picture name. Read the word.
Then underline the two letters that have the **/f/** sound.

1.

trophy

2.

photo

3.

cough

4.
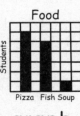
graph

5.

rough

6.

gopher

7.

alphabet

8.

sphere

9.

elephant

Dictation ....

1. cou_____   2. _____oto   3. ele_____ant   4. lau_____

Write It

Word Box

trophy	phone	elephant
alphabet	cough	graph
photo	dolphin	laugh

Write the missing letters to complete the word.
Then read the word.

1.

___ ___ one

2.

tro ___ ___ y

3.

cou ___ ___

4.

dol ___ ___ in

5.

___ ___ oto

6.

ele ___ ___ ant

7.

gra ___ ___

8.

lau ___ ___

9.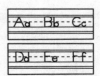

al ___ ___ abet

Dictation

1. enou ___ ___   2. rou ___ ___   3. tro ___ ___ y   4. ___ ___ oto

Listen for It

Focus The letter pairs **ck** and **ng** are digraphs. The **ck** digraph has the /k/ sound. The **ng** digraph has the sound you hear at the end of **ring**. Many words end with these digraphs.

ck		clo**ck**	ng		ri**ng**

Say the picture name.
Then fill in the circle next to the digraph you hear at the **end** of the word.

1.   ○ ck
   ○ ng

2.   ○ ck
   ○ ng

3.   ○ ck
   ○ ng

4.   ○ ck
   ○ ng

5.   ○ ck
   ○ ng

6.    ○ ck
   ○ ng

7.    ○ ck
   ○ ng

8.    ○ ck
   ○ ng

9.   ○ ck
   ○ ng

Dictation ·

1. _____   2. _____   3. _____   4. _____

Write It

Word Box

king	brick	lung
neck	clock	lock
ring	sing	truck

Say the picture name. Then write the word that names the picture.

1.
_____

2.
_____

3.
_____

4.
_____

5.
_____

6.
_____

7.
_____

8.
_____

9.
_____

Dictation

1. _____ 2. _____ 3. _____ 4. _____

Read It

Write the words that complete the sentence.
Then read the sentence.

1. | sang   song   sing |

   Which _____ did she _____?

2. | bang   sock   hang |

   I will _____ my wet _____ to dry.

3. | sting   neck   brick |

   Mick has a bee _____ on his _____.

4. | belong   along   dolphin |

   Does a _____ _____ in a tank?

5. | laugh   photo   tough |

   This _____ of me will make you _____!

Dictation ....

_____

Listen for It

Focus The letters **dge** at the end of a word have the /j/ sound.

ba**dge**

Say the picture name.
Fill in the circle next to **yes** if the final sound is /j/.
Fill in the circle next to **no** if the final sound is <u>not</u> /j/.

1.  ○ yes ○ no	2. ○ yes ○ no	3. ○ yes ○ no
4.  ○ yes ○ no	5.  ○ yes ○ no	6.  ○ yes ○ no
7.  ○ yes ○ no	8. ○ yes ○ no	9.  ○ yes ○ no

Dictation ••

1. _____dge   2. _____dge   3. _____dge   4. _____dge

Write It

Word Box

badge	fudge	nudge
bridge	hedge	pledge
fridge	judge	wedge

Say the picture name. Then write the word on the line.

1.

   _____

2.

   _____

3.

   _____

4.

   _____

5.

   _____

6.

   _____

7.

   _____

8.

   _____

9.

   _____

Dictation

1. ___dge   2. _____dge   3. _____dge   4. _____dge

Listen for It

Focus The sound /ch/ can be spelled with the letters **tch**.

wa**tch**

Say the picture name.
Fill in the circle next to **yes** if the final sound is **/ch/**.
Fill in the circle next to **no** if the final sound is <u>not</u> **/ch/**.

1.

○ yes   ○ no

2.

○ yes   ○ no

3.

○ yes   ○ no

4.

○ yes   ○ no

5.

○ yes   ○ no

6.

○ yes   ○ no

7.

○ yes   ○ no

8.

○ yes   ○ no

9.

○ yes   ○ no

Dictation ....

1. ___ ___tch   2. ___ ___tch   3. ___ ___ ___ ___tch

Write It

Word Box

catch	hatch	pitch
crutch	itch	switch
ditch	kitchen	witch

Say the picture name. Then write the word on the line.

1.
_____

2.
_____

3.
_____

4.
_____

5.
_____

6.
_____

7.
_____

8.
_____

9.
_____

Dictation ••

_____

Read It

Write the word that completes the sentence.
Then read the sentence out loud.

1. Is the _____ in the fridge?

   nudge   fudge

2. You _____ the ball, and I will catch it.

   patch   pitch

3. A _____ gave me a trophy at the end of the match.

   judge   budge

4. My dog will _____ the stick by the hedge.

   sketch   fetch

5. Do not stand at the _____ of the ledge.

   badge   edge

6. Does your badge _____ my badge?

   match   hatch

Dictation ••

_____

Daily Phonics • EMC 6773 • © Evan-Moor Corp.

Listen for It

Focus   Sometimes a consonant is **silent**, or does not have a sound.
In words beginning with **kn**, the **k** is usually silent.
In words beginning with **wr**, the **w** is usually silent.

knee   **w**rite

Say the picture name. Listen to the letter-sounds.
Then cross out the **silent** consonant in the word.

1.	2.	3.
knot	wrap	kneel
4.	**5.**	**6.**
wrist	knife	knock
7.	**8.**	**9.**
knit	wreck	wrench

Dictation •

1. k_____   2. w_____   3. w_____

Listen for It

Focus   Sometimes the consonants **b** and **h** are **silent**.

com**b**		r**h**yme	

Say the picture name. Listen to the letter-sounds.
Then cross out the **silent** consonant in the word.

1.	2.	3.
lamb	ghost	thumb

4.	5.	6.
hour	limb	crumb

7.	8.	9.
 climb	 rhino	 plumber

Dictation •

1. _____   2. _____   3. _____

Listen for It

Focus   When the letter l comes before **f**, **v**, or **k**, the l can be silent.

calf
ca~~l~~f

Say the picture name. Listen to the letter-sounds.
Then cross out the **silent** consonant in the word.

1.  walk	2. half	3.  yolk
4.  calves	5. chalk	6. polka dot
7.  talk	8.  stalk	9. halves

Dictation ···

1. _____   2. _____   3. _____

Write It

Word Box

thumb	rhino	yolk
wrap	knit	comb
walk	knee	talk

Say the picture name. Then write the word on the line.

1.

_____

2.

_____

3.

_____

4.

_____

5.

_____

6.

_____

7.

_____

8.

_____

9.

_____

Dictation

1. _____   2. _____   3. _____

Read It

Write the words that complete the sentence.
Then read the sentence out loud.

1.　　half　　calf　　knife

   Use a _____ to cut the cake in _____.

2.　　climb　　walk　　crumb

   You can _____ up the path and _____ the hill.

3.　　crumb　　lamb　　thumb

   Pick up the _____ with your _____.

4.　　wrote　　chalk　　wrap

   Anna _____ her name with white _____.

5.　　knot　　rhino　　knock

   A _____ can _____ down a tree!

Dictation ⋯⋯⋯⋯⋯⋯⋯⋯⋯⋯⋯⋯⋯⋯⋯⋯⋯⋯⋯⋯⋯⋯⋯⋯

_____

Listen for It

Focus The vowel pairs **ai** and **ay** are digraphs that have the **long a** sound. The vowels **ai** usually come in the **middle** of a word. The vowels **ay** usually come at the **end** of a word.

long **a**

ta**i**l | tr**ay**

Say the picture name. Read the word.
Then underline the two letters that stand for the **long a** sound.

1. nail	2. hay	3. rain
4. mail	5. clay	6. brain
7. snail	8. paid	9. X-ray

Dictation ··

1. _____   2. _____   3. _____

Listen for It

Letter Box

ai   ay

Say the picture name.
Then write the letters that spell the word.

1. t ___ l	2. cl ___	3. r ___ n
4. tr ___ n	5. n ___ l	6. sn ___ l
7. j ___	8. p ___ nt	9.  subw ___
10. m ___ l	11. ch ___ n	12. br ___ d

Dictation

1. _____   2. _____   3. _____

Write It

Word Box

paint	tray	pay
jay	braid	pail
freeway	chain	trail

Say the picture name. Write the word on the line.
Then circle the letters that have the **long a** sound.

1.
_____

2.
_____

3.
_____

4.
_____

5.
_____

6.
_____

7.
_____

8.
_____

9.
_____

Dictation

1. _____   2. _____   3. _____

Read It

Read the phrase. Underline the letters that have the **long a** sound.
Then draw a line from the words to the correct picture.

1. stack of **hay**

2. **rainy day**

3. **train** on a track

4. **spray paint**

5. tree by the **trail**

6. thick **braid**

7. **freeway** to the city

Dictation ••

Read It

Write the word that completes each sentence.
Then read the sentence out loud.

1. This toy train is made from _____.
   play   clay

2. Jay likes to chase me in the _____.
   hallway   freeway

3. The snail left a _____ of slime.
   train   trail

4. May I hang my hat on that _____?
   hail   nail

5. How did the dog get _____ on its tail?
   pain   paint

6. I am not afraid to _____ on the lake.
   sail   stain

Dictation ....

_____

Daily Phonics • EMC 6773 • © Evan-Moor Corp.

Listen for It

Focus The vowel pairs **ee** and **ea** are digraphs that often have the **long e** sound.

long **e**

qu**ee**n   j**ea**ns

Say the picture name. Read the word.
Then underline the two letters that stand for the **long e** sound.

1. seal	2. feet	3. jeep
4. bean	5. leaf	6. kneel
7. peach	8. sneeze	9. team

Dictation ••

1. ea_____   2. ____ee____   3. ____ea_____

Listen for It

Focus The vowel pairs **ey** and **ie** are digraphs that often have the **long e** sound. The digraph **ey** usually comes at the **end** of a word. The digraph **ie** usually comes in the **middle** of a word.

long **e**

jo**ey** chi**e**f

Say the picture name. Read the word.
Then underline the two letters that stand for the **long e** sound.

1. key	2. donkey	3. thief
4. money	5. field	6. monkey
7. honey	8. piece	9. shield

Dictation ....

1. ___ ___ie___   2. ___ey   3. ___ ___ie___

Read It

Read each pair of words. Underline the letters that have the **long e** sound.
Then draw a line to the correct picture.

1. white **bean**

2. **sweet honey**

3. big **sneeze**

4. **green field**

5. **deep sleep**

6. sandy **beach**

7. my **team**

8. little **joey**

Dictation ....

1. ___ ___ie___   2. ___ ___ee___   3. ___ea___ ___   4. ___ ___ ___ey

Write It

Word Box

beach	jeep	chief
donkey	honey	peek
piece	seal	sweep

Write the word that names the picture.
Then circle the two letters that stand for the **long e** sound.

1.

_____

2.

_____

3.

_____

4.

_____

5.

_____

6.

_____

7.

_____

8.

_____

9.

_____

Dictation

1. ___ea_____   2. _____ey   3. _____ee___   4. _____ie_____

Read It

Word Box

chief	dream	freeze	jeep
money	monkey	peach	piece

Write the word that completes the sentence.
Then read the sentence out loud.

1. A thief may steal all of your _____.

2. A _____ is sweet to eat.

3. A _____ leads a team.

4. Ice cream will melt if you do not _____ it.

5. A _____ can hang from its tail.

6. You _____ when you sleep.

7. I drive my _____ on the field.

8. You can eat a _____ of cheese.

Dictation ....

_____

Listen for It

Focus The letters **ie** and **igh** can have the **long i** sound.

long i	
t**ie**	h**igh**

Say the picture name. Read the word.
Then underline the letters that stand for the **long i** sound.

1. pie	2. light	3. fight
4. high	5.  lie	6. thigh
7. fried	8. night	9. cries

Dictation ....

1. ___igh___   2. _____ie___   3. ___ ___igh___

Write It

Word Box

night	tie	tried	light
fried	thigh	high	pie
bright	lie	cries	right

Read each word. Then write it under **ie** or **igh**.

ie	igh
_____	_____
_____	_____
_____	_____
_____	_____
_____	_____
_____	_____

Dictation

1. _____ie____   2. ___igh____   3. _____igh___

Write It

Word Box

cries	fight	fried
night	high	light
lie	thigh	pie

Write the word that names the picture.
Then circle the letters that stand for the **long i** sound.

1.

_____

2.

_____

3.

_____

4.

_____

5.

_____

6.

_____

7.

_____

8.

_____

9.

_____

Dictation

1. ___ ___ie___ 2. ___igh___ 3. ___igh___

Daily Phonics • EMC 6773 • © Evan-Moor Corp.

Read It

Say the picture name.
Then fill in the circle next to the word that names the picture.

1.	2. 	3.
○ fries　　○ flies	○ night　　○ tight	○ right　　○ night
4. 	5.	6.
○ tries　　○ spies	○ dries　　○ cries	○ tights　　○ lights
7.	8.	9.
○ thigh　　○ high	○ tied　　○ tried	○ bright　　○ fright
10. 	11. 	12. 
○ lie　　○ tie	○ sight　　○ light	○ fried　　○ cried

Dictation ••

1. _____ie___　　2. _____ie___　　3. _____igh___

Read It

Write the words that complete the sentence.
Then read the sentence out loud.

1.

   bright   light   sight

   My desk _____ is too _____.

2.

   tried   cried   spies

   The _____ _____ to catch the thief.

3.

   fried   fries   flies

   Keep the _____ away from my _____!

4.

   right   tie   night

   What is the _____ way to _____ a knot?

5.

   tights   sunlight   cried   dried

   I _____ my _____ in the _____.

Dictation ••

_____

Listen for It

Focus — The vowel pairs **oa** and **oe** are digraphs that usually have the **long o** sound.

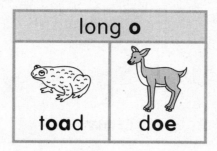

long **o**	
t**oa**d	d**oe**

Say the picture name. Read the word.
Then underline the two vowels that stand for the **long o** sound.

1. road	2. toe	3.  loaf
4. soap	5. hoe	6. foam
7. coach	8.  boat	9. toast

Dictation ••

1. ___oa___   2. ___oe   3. ___oa___

Listen for It

Focus   The letter pair **ow** is a digraph that can have the **long o** sound.

long o

cr**ow**

Say the picture name. Read the word.
Then underline the two letters that stand for the **long o** sound.

1. mow	2.  tow	3.  row
4. crow	5.  throw	6. window
7. bowl	8. snow	9. grown

Dictation ••

1. g____ow   2. _____ow   3. _____ow   4. _____ow

Write It

Word Box

bowl	coach	float
loaf	soap	rainbow
row	throw	toes

Say the picture name. Write the word on the line.
Then circle the letters that have the **long o** sound.

1.

_____

2.

_____

3.

_____

4.

_____

5.

_____

6.

_____

7.

_____

8.

_____

9.

_____

Dictation

1. ___oe___   2. ___oa___   3. _____ow   4. _____ow___

Read It

Read the phrase. Underline the words that have the **long o** sound.
Then draw a line from the words to the correct picture.

1. a toe with a bow

2. a goat on a road

3. a coach who mows

4. a toad that croaks

5. blowing snow

6. a coat to loan

7. a bowl of oats

Dictation

1. _____   2. _____   3. _____   4. _____

Read It

Write the word that completes the sentence.
Then read the sentence out loud.

1. Do you _____ how to row a boat?
   knot   know

2. Joe knows how to _____ a baseball.
   throw   throat

3. Goats eat on the hill _____ our home.
   window   below

4. A doe was next to the old _____ tree.
   oak   boat

5. Please show me how to _____.
   float   flown

6. I will _____ you my yellow coat.
   load   loan

Dictation •••

_____

Listen for It

Focus The letter pairs **ew** and **ue** are digraphs that usually have the **long u** sound.

long **u**

n**ew**   cl**ue**

Say the picture name. Read the word.
Then underline the two letters that stand for the **long u** sound.

1. fuel	2. flew	3. chew
4. blue	5. grew	6. glue
7. Sue	8. jewel	9. Tuesday

Dictation ••

1. ___ew___   2. _____ew   3. _____ue   4. _____ue

Daily Phonics • EMC 6773 • © Evan-Moor Corp.

Write It

Word Box

flew	grew	clue	Tuesday
stew	blue	hue	chew
glue	due	screw	jewel

Read each word. Then write it under the correct letter pair.

ew	ue
_____	_____
_____	_____
_____	_____
_____	_____
_____	_____
_____	_____

Dictation ···

1. ___ ___ew   2. _____ue   3. _____ew   4. ___ue

Write It

Word Box

blew	blue	fuel
glue	grew	jewel
stew	threw	Tuesday

Say the picture name. Write the word on the line.
Then circle the letters that have the **long u** sound.

1.
_____

2.
_____

3.
_____

4.
_____

5.
_____

6.
_____

7.
_____

8.
_____

9.
_____

Dictation

1. _____   2. _____   3. _____

Read It

Read each phrase. Underline the word or words that have the **long u** sound.
Then draw a line to the correct picture.

1. true blue

2. a bone to chew

3. fuel for a car

4. a pot of stew

5. a jewel on a ring

6. a few screws

7. a plant that grew

Dictation ....

1. _____   2. _____

Read It

Write the words that complete the sentence.
Then read the sentence out loud.

1.

   new   flew   stew

   Dad made _____ in the _____ pot.

2.

   glue   blue   drew

   I _____ with puffy _____ .

3.

   few   news   chews

   Buddy _____ a _____ bones each day.

4.

   fuel   true   news

   The _____ about Sue is _____ .

5.

   threw   true   screws

   Mom _____ the _____ into the bag.

Dictation ••

_____

Daily Phonics • EMC 6773 • © Evan-Moor Corp.

Listen for It

Focus The vowel digraph **ea** sometimes has the **short e** sound.

short **e**

h**ea**d

Say the picture name. Then read the word.
Does it have the **short e** sound? Fill in the circle next to **yes** or **no**.

1. bread ○ yes no	2. seal yes ○ no	3. feather ○ yes no
4. spread ○ yes ○ no	5. sweat ○ yes ○ no	6. peach ○ yes ○ no
7. bean yes ○ no	8. thread ○ yes ○ no	9. sweater ○ yes no

Dictation •

1. ___ea___   2. ___ea____   3. ___ea___

Write It

Word Box

sweat	bread	head
read	ready	sweater

Write the word that completes the sentence.

1. 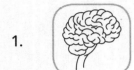 Your brain is inside your _____.

2.  Do you like to eat wheat _____?

3.  The hot sun makes me _____.

4. 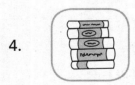 I _____ five books last week.

5.  My _____ is too tight for me.

6.  Kate is _____ to bake a cake.

Dictation

1. _____   2. _____   3. _____

Listen for It

Focus — The vowel pair **ou** is a digraph that can have the **short u** sound.

short **u**

touch

Read the word. Does it have the **short u** sound?
Fill in the circle next to **yes** or **no**.

1.

young

○ yes   ○ no

2.

shoe

○ yes   ○ no

3.

rough

○ yes   ○ no

4.

glue

yes   ○ no

5.

cousins

○ yes   no

6.

country

○ yes   ○ no

7.

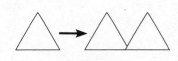

double

○ yes   ○ no

8.

moon

○ yes   ○ no

9.

couple

○ yes   ○ no

Dictation ••

1. ___ou_____   2. ___ou_____   3. ___ou_____

Write It

Word Box

country	cousin	enough
rough	touch	young

Write the word that completes the sentence.

1. A brick wall feels _____.

2. I live in a very large _____.

3. I am _____, but Gramps is not.

4. My cat is soft to _____.

5. You must try to get _____ sleep.

6. My _____ and I are the same age.

Dictation

1. _____   2. _____   3. _____

Daily Phonics • EMC 6773 • © Evan-Moor Corp.

Read It

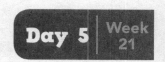

Write the word that completes the sentence.
Then read the sentence out loud.

1. The meat in this stew is too _____ to chew.

   enough   tough

2. Joe is _____ in the race.

   ahead   head

3. If you _____ the hot stove, you will be in trouble!

   tough   touch

4. I have a young _____ named Doug.

   cousin   country

5. The baby bird is _____ to grow feathers.

   read   ready

6. I like to spread jam on _____.

   braid   bread

Dictation ....

_____

Listen for It

Focus The vowel pair **oo** is a digraph that can have the sound you hear in **boot**. It can also have the sound you hear in **hook**.

boot   hook

Say the picture name. Listen to the vowel sound. Then name each picture in the row. Fill in the circle if it has the same vowel sound as the first picture.

1.    ○   ○   ○

2. 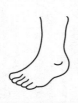   ○   ○   ○

3.    ○   ○   ○

4.   ○    ○   ○

Dictation ·

1. _____   2. _____   3. _____

   Daily Phonics • EMC 6773 • © Evan-Moor Corp.

Write It

Word Box

brook	cook	food
goose	hood	root
spoon	tooth	zoo

Say the picture name.
Write the word on the line.

1.

_____

2.

_____

3.

_____

4.

_____

5.

_____

6.

_____

7.

_____

8.

_____

9.

_____

Dictation ....

1. _____   2. _____   3. _____   4. _____

Write It

Word Box

book	cool	football	good	moon
pool	snoop	stood	shoot	wood

Read each word in the box above.
Then write it under the word in bold type that has the same **oo** sound.

long	short
pool	**wood**
_____	_____
_____	_____
_____	_____
_____	_____
_____	_____

Dictation ....

1. _____   2. _____   3. _____   4. _____

Read It

Read the phrase. Underline the words that have the vowel sound in **broom**.
Circle the words that have the vowel sound in **wood**.
Then draw a line to the correct picture.

1. a **moose** on the **loose**

2. **spoons** for the **cook**

3. a deep **pool**

4. a **good book**

5. the yellow **moon**

6. a pile of **wood**

Dictation ....

The _____ of a _____ is called a _____.

Read It

Write the words that complete the sentence.
Then read the sentence out loud.

1.

   wood   cook   spoon

   The _____ is made of _____.

2.

   zoo   goose   moose

   The _____ flew into the _____.

3.

   cool   fool   pool

   I need to _____ off in the _____.

4.

   foot   mood   boot

   That _____ is too big for my _____.

5.

   room   boom   broom

   I need a _____ to sweep my _____.

Dictation ··

_____

Listen for It

Focus The letter pairs **au** and **aw** are digraphs that can have the vowel sound you hear in **haul** and **claw**.

h**au**l    cl**aw**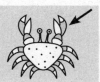

Say the picture name. Read the word.
Then underline the letters that stand for the vowel sound you hear in **raw**.

1. 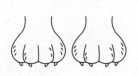 paws	2. hawk	3. sauce
4. caught	5. yawn	6. August
7.  straw	8.  faucet	9.  seesaw

Dictation ···

1. ___au___ ___   2. ___aw___   3. ___au___   4. ___ ___aw

Write It

Word Box

pause	straw	fawn	haunt	fault
faucet	jaw	paws	draw	sauce

Read each word in the box above.
Then write the word under the correct letter pair.

au	aw
_____	_____
_____	_____
_____	_____
_____	_____
_____	_____

Dictation •••

1. ___aw___   2. ___au_____   3. ___au_____   4. _____aw

Daily Phonics • EMC 6773 • © Evan-Moor Corp.

Write It

Word Box

claw	draw	faucet
fawn	haunt	jaw
hawk	paws	vault

Say the picture name. Write the word on the line.
Then circle the letters that stand for the **/aw/** sound.

1.
_____

2.
_____

3.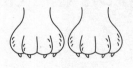
_____

4.
_____

5.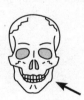
_____

6.
_____

7.
_____

8.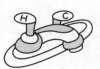
_____

9.
_____

Dictation

....

_____

Read It

Read the phrase. Underline the letters that have the **/aw/** sound.
Then draw a line from the words to the correct picture.

1. a big **yawn**

2. a **lawn** with a path

3. **paws** with **claws**

4. a bank **vault**

5. a bent **straw**

6. **sauce** to eat

7. a **hawk** that **squawks**

8. a cup and **saucer**

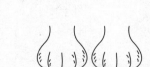

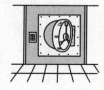

Dictation ··

Read It

Write the word that completes the sentence.
Then read the sentence out loud.

1. I saw a _____ and a doe on our lawn.
   fun   fawn

2. A hawk grabs food with its _____.
   clues   claws

3. The truck will _____ the pile of straw away.
   haul   hole

4. We will _____ the rocket at dawn.
   launch   lunch

5. What caused you to _____ in class?
   haul   yawn

6. My cat will lick his _____.
   peas   paws

Dictation ....

_____

Listen for It

Focus The letter pairs **ou** and **ow** sometimes have the vowel sound you hear in **cloud** and in **clown**.

cloud 	**clow**n

Say the picture name. Then read the word.
Circle the letters that stand for the vowel sound you hear in **how**.

1.

bow

2.

mouse

3.

gown

4.

crown

5.

flour

6.

flower

7.

mouth

8.

couch

9.

owl

Dictation ....

1. ___ou___   2. ___ ___ou___   3. ___ow___   4. ___ ___ow___

   Daily Phonics • EMC 6773 • © Evan-Moor Corp.

Write It

Word Box

cloud	couch	crowd
down	flour	frown
mouth	scout	tower

Say the picture name. Write the word on the line.
Then circle the letters that have the vowel sound you hear in **clown**.

1.

_____

2.

_____

3.

_____

4.

_____

5.

_____

6.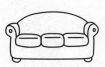

_____

7.

_____

8.

_____

9.

_____

Dictation

1. ____ou____   2. ____ou____   3. _____ow   4. ____ow____

Listen for It

Focus The letter pairs **oi** and **oy** have the vowel sound you hear in **coins** and in **toy**. The letter pair **oi** usually comes in the middle of a word. The letter pair **oy** usually comes at the end of a word.

| coins | | toy | |

Say the picture name. Then read the word.
Underline the letters that stand for the vowel sound you hear in **boy**.

1.	2.	3.
boy	coin	oil
4.	5.	6.
joy	cowboy	soil
7.	8.	9.
coil	toys	point

Dictation ••

1. _____   2. _____   3. _____

Write It

Word Box

toys	boil	coins	cowboy
coil	point	joy	soil

Read the clue. Then write the correct word on the line.

1. round money _____

2. a man on a ranch _____

3. a place for a plant _____

4. to show where to go _____

5. to go around and around _____

6. a way to cook _____

7. fun to play with _____

8. a happy feeling _____

Dictation ···

_____

Read It

Write the words that complete the sentence.
Then read the sentence out loud.

1. oil   boil   flour

   You can mix the wheat _____ with the _____.

2. gown   clown   toy

   The _____ gave Roy a funny _____.

3. soil   flowers   soy

   Will _____ grow in this rocky _____?

4. joy   join   scout

   I will _____ a _____ troop in the fall.

5. mouse   town   couch

   Did you see a _____ run under the _____?

Dictation •••

_____

Listen for It

Focus When a vowel is followed by the letter **r**, the **r** changes the sound of the vowel. The sounds blend to make a new sound.

ar		or	
b**ar**n		c**or**n	

Say the picture name. Fill in the circle next to the letters that stand for the **vowel + r** sound you hear.

1.   ○ ar ○ or

2.  ○ ar ○ or

3.   ○ ar ○ or

4.   ○ ar ○ or

5.  ○ ar ○ or

6.   ○ ar ○ or

7.  ○ ar ○ or

8.  ○ ar ○ or

9. Get Well! ○ ar ○ or

Dictation ....

1. _____   2. _____   3. _____   4. _____

Write It

Letter Box

ar · or

Say the picture name.
Then write the missing letters to spell the word.

1.

c __ __ d

2.

f __ __ k

3.

b __ __ n

4.

p __ __ k

5.

c __ __ n

6.

h __ __ n

7.

m __ __ ch

8.

st __ __ m

9.

p __ __ ty

Dictation

1. _____   2. _____   3. _____   4. _____

Listen for It

Focus When an **e**, an **i**, or a **u** is followed by an **r**, the vowel sound blends with the **r** to make a new sound. The letter pairs **er**, **ir**, and **ur** have the same sound you hear in **fur**.

person   dirt   burn

Say the picture name. Then read the word.
Underline the letters that have the **vowel + r** sound you hear in **fur**.

1.	2.	3.
girl	turtle	purse
4.	5.	6.
herd	thirty	turkey
7.	8.	9.
river	skirt	spider

Dictation ···

1. _____ur_____   2. _____er_____   3. _____ir_____

Write It

Word Box

dirty	herd	curb	purse
spider	stir	turkey	under

Read each word in the box above. Underline the letters that stand for the **vowel + r** sound. Then read each definition below and write the word that goes with it.

1. below _____

2. to mix _____

3. a kind of bird _____

4. spins a web _____

5. not clean _____

6. a group of cows _____

7. side of the road _____

8. a bag for a lady _____

Dictation ••

1. ___ur___   2. _____er   3. ___ir_____

Read It

Write the word that completes the sentence.
Then read the sentence out loud.

1. The _____ lit up the dark sky.
   stars   stirs

2. The horse must stay in the _____.
   burn   barn

3. It is your _____ to feed the bird.
   turn   torn

4. What _____ do you play at the park?
   spurt   sport

5. We have a _____ of thirty cows.
   hard   herd

6. Burt is washing the _____ off his arm.
   dirt   dart

Dictation ••

_____

Listen for It

Focus The letter combinations **air** and **are** have the **vowel + r** sound you hear in **fair**.

fair | share

Say the picture name. Read the word.
Then underline the letters that have the **r + vowel** sound you hear in **fair**.

1.  mare	2.  hair	3.  stares
4. chair	5.  scare	6. pair
7. stairs	8. hare	9.  share

Dictation •••

1. ___ai___   2. ___are   3. _____air___   4. ___are

Write It

Word Box

hare	chair	hair
mare	pair	square
scare	share	stairs

Say the picture name. Write the word on the line.
Then circle the letters with the **vowel + r** sound.

1.

_____

2.

_____

3.

_____

4.

_____

5.

_____

6.

_____

7.

_____

8.

_____

9.

_____

Dictation ••

1. ____ ____are   2. air____ ____ ____   3. ____ ____air____ ____

Listen for It

Focus When the vowel pair **ea** is followed by an **r**, it often has the **vowel + r** sound you hear in **ear**. It can also have the **vowel + r** sound you hear in **bear**.

| ear | | bear | |

Read the sentence. Say the word in bold type. Circle the word if it has the **vowel + r** sound in **ear**. Underline the word if it has the **vowel + r** sound in **bear**.

1. You **hear** with your ear.

2. You **wear** a sweater.

3. You eat a **pear**.

4. You cry **tears** when you are sad.

5. If you stand next to me, you stand **near**.

6. If you rip your pants, you **tear** them.

7. You see inside a **clear** glass.

8. You stay away from a **bear**.

Dictation ....

1. ___ear   2. ___ear   3. _____ear   4. _____ear

Daily Phonics • EMC 6773 • © Evan-Moor Corp.

Write It

Word Box

bear	chair	clear
hair	fair	pear
square	stare	tears

Say the picture name. Then write the word on the line.

1.

_____

2.

_____

3.

_____

4.

_____

5.

_____

6.

_____

7.

_____

8.

_____

9.

_____

Dictation

_____

Read It

Write the words that complete the sentence.
Then read the sentence out loud.

1.   mare   dare   care

   Clare will take _____ of the old _____.

2.   pear   share   scare

   I will _____ my _____ with you.

3.   clear   care   stare

   I like to _____ at the _____ blue sky.

4.   fair   stairs   chair

   Please put the _____ at the top of the _____.

5.   near   pair   bear

   Do not go _____ the _____ and her cubs.

Dictation ••

_____

Read It

Focus When a word has an **s** added to the end, it shows more than one. The **s** makes the word plural. The **s** can have the /s/ or /z/ sound.

 bear + **s** = bears

Look at the picture. Read the words.
Then fill in the circle next to the correct word.

1. ○ nut ○ nuts	2. ○ hawk ○ hawks	3. ○ cake ○ cakes
4. ○ chain ○ chains	5. ○ mask ○ masks	6. ○ comb ○ combs
7.  ○ chair ○ chairs	8. ○ skunk ○ skunks	9. ○ clown ○ clowns

Dictation ••

1. _____   2. _____   3. _____   4. _____

Write It

Focus Some words have **es** added to the end to make them plural. An **es** is added to words that end in **ch**, **sh**, **ss**, or **x**.

| peach**es** | dish**es** | dress**es** | fox**es** |

Look at the picture. Read the word.
Then write the **plural** form of the word on the line.

1.

box

_____

2.

dish

_____

3.

couch

_____

4.

glass

_____

5.

brush

_____

6.

lunch

_____

Dictation ....

1. _____   2. _____   3. _____

Write It

Focus When a word ends in a **consonant** and a **y**, the **y** is changed to **ies** to make the word plural. The letter **s** has the **/z/** sound.

| fly | fly + **ies** = flies | flies |

Make the word plural. Change the **y** to **ies**.
Then read the word you wrote.

1.

spy

_____

2.

pony

_____

3.

berry

_____

4.

candy

_____

5.

cherry

_____

6.

penny

_____

7.

puppy

_____

8.

lady

_____

9.

fry

_____

Dictation •

1. _____ _____   2. _____ _____

Write It

Focus When a word ends in **f**, the **f** is changed to **ves** to make the word plural.

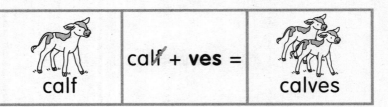

calf | cal̸f + **ves** = | calves

Make the word plural. Change the **f** to **v** and add **es**.
Then read the word you wrote.

1.

elf

_____

2.

half

_____

3.

loaf

_____

4.

scarf

_____

5.

wolf

_____

6.

leaf

_____

7.

shelf

_____

8.

thief

_____

9.

knife

_____

Dictation ....

1. _____ _____   2. _____ _____

Read It

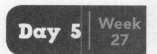

Word Box

cookies	foxes	dishes	flies
peaches	scarves	spies	kisses

Write the word that completes the sentence.
Then read the sentence out loud.

1. The _____ wore dark glasses.

2. Our new set of cups and _____ came in big boxes.

3. Wolves and _____ have bushy tails.

4. Big black _____ buzzed around the ponies.

5. Cherries, plums, and _____ have pits.

6. Mom gave the babies many hugs and _____.

7. I will bake two batches of yummy _____.

8. The ladies have new red dresses and _____.

Dictation ••

_____

Listen for It

Focus | Some plural forms of words are very different from their singular forms. The vowels might change or the whole word might change.

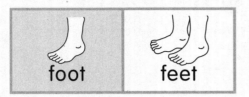

foot | feet

child | children

Read the word. Then draw a line to its plural form.

1. man   • people

2. woman   • teeth

3. goose   • mice

4. tooth   • women

5. mouse   • men

6. person   • geese

Dictation •

1. man _____   2. tooth _____   3. mouse _____

Write It

Word Box

mouse	teeth	feet	foot
geese	child	woman	children
tooth	women	mice	goose

Read each word in the box above. If the word is singular, write it under **one**.
If the word is plural, write it under **more than one**.

singular **one**	plural **more than one**
_____	_____
_____	_____
_____	_____
_____	_____
_____	_____
_____	_____

Dictation •

_____

Write It

Focus   Some words have the same singular and plural forms. The spellings do not change.

deer   deer

jeans   jeans

The words in bold type have the same singular and plural forms.
Write the plural form of the word on the line.

1. one **sheep**   a flock of _____

2. black **pants**   two pairs of _____

3. a **moose**   three _____

4. one **deer**   many _____

5. my **glasses**   some cute _____

6. a pair of **shorts**   two pairs of _____

Dictation •••

1. _____   2. _____   3. _____   4. _____

Write It

Read the first pair of words in each row. Then write the plural form of the word that appears in bold type.

1. one **mouse**   many _____

2. my **shorts**   these _____

3. a **man**   a group of _____

4. your **foot**   your _____

5. a **deer**   a herd of _____

6. one **tooth**   many _____

7. one **child**   four _____

Dictation ....

_____

Read It

Write the word that completes the sentence.
Then read the sentence out loud.

1. Some of the _____ wore sunglasses.

   man   men

2. Geese do not have _____.

   tooth   teeth

3. Five deer ran past three _____.

   moose   meese

4. All the _____ fled when they saw the mice.

   person   people

5. These socks are too big for my _____.

   foot   feet

6. Many _____ tried on jeans at the store.

   women   woman

Dictation ••

_____

Write It

Focus Most verbs are action words. When a verb ends in **ed**, it means the action has already happened. When a verb ends with **ing**, it means the action is or was in the process of happening.

action	+ **ed**	+ **ing**
I help.	I help**ed**.	I am help**ing**.
		I was help**ing**.

Read the action word. Write it with each ending.
Then read the new words you wrote. Listen for the sound **ed** has in each word.

action (base word)	+ **ed**	+ **ing**
1. ask	_____	_____
2. turn	_____	_____
3. pass	_____	_____
4. grill	_____	_____
5. end	_____	_____
6. visit	_____	_____
7. paint	_____	_____

Dictation •

1. _____   2. _____   3. _____

Write It

Focus When a verb ends with a **silent e**, you drop the **e** before adding **ed** or **ing**. The first vowel in the verb has a long sound.

action	+ ed	+ ing
I hike.	I hik**ed**.	I am hik**ing**. I was hik**ing**.

Read the action word. Then write the word and follow the rule to add **ed**. Write the word again and follow the rule to add **ing**.

action (base word)	+ ed	+ ing
1. joke	_____	_____
2. wave	_____	_____
3. hope	_____	_____
4. wipe	_____	_____
5. fade	_____	_____
6. chase	_____	_____
7. skate	_____	_____

Dictation •

1. _____ 2. _____ 3. _____

Write It

Focus When a verb ends with one short vowel and one consonant, the final consonant is doubled before **ing** or **ed** is added. The first vowel has a short sound.

action	+ **ed**	+ **ing**
I jog.	I jogg**ed**.	I am jogg**ing**. I was jogg**ing**.

Read the action word. Then write the word and follow the rule to add **ed**.
Write the word again and follow the rule to add **ing**.

action (base word)	+ **ed**	+ **ing**
1. rip	_____	_____
2. flip	_____	_____
3. brag	_____	_____
4. grin	_____	_____
5. drop	_____	_____
6. plan	_____	_____
7. skid	_____	_____

Dictation ....

1. _____   2. _____   3. _____

Write It

Focus Sometimes a verb has an **s** or an **es** added to it. You add an **s** when a verb ends in a **consonant** or a **silent e**. You add **es** when a verb ends in **ch**, **sh**, **ss**, or **x**. The **es** sounds like /ĭz/.

gra**b** grab**s**	rea**ch** reach**es**	pu**sh** push**es**	mi**ss** miss**es**	mi**x** mix**es**

Read the word. Then write the word and follow the rule to add **s or es**.
Read the new word you wrote.

1. toss _____	2. fix _____	3. wash _____
4. jump _____	5. itch _____	6. pass _____
7. rush _____	8. drop _____	9. watch _____

Dictation ∙∙∙

1. _____   2. _____   3. _____

Read It

Write the words that complete the sentence.
Then read the sentence out loud.

1. washed   hummed   jumped

   Ray _____ as he _____ the dishes.

2. tossed   dropped   slipped

   I _____ the ball to Jacob, but he _____ it.

3. itching   itches   wishes

   Chad _____ his bug bite would stop _____.

4. flipped   ripped   hummed

   Ava _____ her jeans when she _____ over.

5. joining   planning   wishing

   Rosa is _____ on _____ us today.

Dictation ....

_____

Read It

Focus A **contraction** is a short way of writing two words. An **apostrophe** shows that one or more letters has been left out. Many contractions are formed using the verbs **is** or **are**.

| that ~~is~~ = that's | you ~~are~~ = you're |

Read the contraction. Then write the two words that form the contraction.

1. it's _____   6. how's _____

2. he's _____   7. we're _____

3. they're _____   8. she's _____

4. here's _____   9. what's _____

5. who's _____   10. where's _____

Dictation •

1. _____   2. _____   3. _____

Read It

Focus   Many contractions are formed using the verbs **had** or **will**.

I had = I'd	we will = we'll

Read the contraction. Then write the two words that form the contraction.

1. I'll _____

2. you'd _____

3. they'll _____

4. she'll _____

5. that'll _____

6. you'll _____

7. she'd _____

8. we'd _____

9. he'll _____

10. he'd _____

Dictation ···

1. _____   2. _____

Read It

Focus   Many contractions are formed using the adverb **not**.

is not = isn't

Read the contraction. Then write the two words that form the contraction.

1. don't _____

2. can't _____

3. hadn't _____

4. couldn't _____

5. wasn't _____

6. hasn't _____

7. aren't _____

8. weren't _____

Dictation ....

1. _____   2. _____

Read It

Read each pair of words. Draw a line from the words to the correct contraction.
Then read the contraction out loud.

1. does not   • we'll

2. who is   • what's

3. you are   • they're

4. you will   • who's

5. we will   • you'll

6. what is   • you're

7. should not   • doesn't

8. they are   • shouldn't

Dictation

1. was not _____   2. I am _____   3. we are _____

Write It

Write the contraction for each pair of words.
Then read the sentence out loud.

1. Emma _____ know that it's raining.

does not

2. We'll ask Mom if _____ bake cookies.

she will

3. _____ the reason he's late for the game?

what is

4. I'm sure that this _____ the right street.

is not

5. I've washed the car, but _____ done nothing.

you have

6. She's saying that we _____ go with you.

can not

Dictation

1. _____   2. _____

Write It

Focus A prefix is a word part added to the **beginning** of a word. Each prefix has a meaning. Knowing what a prefix means helps you know what a word means.

un = not, or the opposite of
un + kind = **un**kind

re = again
re + play = **re**play

Add each prefix to the beginning of the base word.
Write the two new words on the lines. Then read the words you wrote.

base word	un	re
1. pack	_____	_____
2. tie	_____	_____
3. done	_____	_____
4. cover	_____	_____
5. paid	_____	_____
6. wrap	_____	_____
7. seal	_____	_____
8. load	_____	_____

Dictation ....

1. _____ 2. _____ 3. _____

Write It

Focus — Each prefix has a meaning. Knowing what a prefix means helps you know what a word means.

| **dis** = not | **re** = again | **un** = not, or the opposite of |

Read the word in bold type. Underline the prefix.
Then complete the meaning of the word.

1.
rerun

to _____ again

2.
uneven

not _____

3.
dislike

to not _____

4.
disallow

to not _____

5.
refill

to _____ again

6.
unkind

not _____

7.
unsure

not _____

8.
rewrite

to _____ again

9.
disagree

to not _____

Dictation ••

1. _____   2. _____   3. _____

Write It

dis = not	re = again	un = not, or the opposite of

Read the definition. Write the correct prefix in front of the base word.
Then write the new word.

1. not even   ____even   _____

2. to read again   ____read   _____

3. to paint again   ____paint   _____

4. not happy   ____happy   _____

5. to not agree   ____agree   _____

6. not sure   ____sure   _____

7. to not trust   ____trust   _____

8. to count again   ____count   _____

Dictation •

_____

Write It

Prefix Box

dis   re   un

One word in each sentence is missing a prefix.
Write the correct prefix to complete the word. Then read the sentence.

1. Jan will _____fill the car with gas.

2. I'm _____happy that my dog ate my shoe.

3. Daniel and Megan _____like bananas.

4. We will _____pack our bags after our trip.

5. I'll _____write my messy homework.

6. Mom and I _____agree over my bedtime.

7. My dad will _____paint my bedroom.

Dictation ···

_____

Read It

Write the word that completes the sentence.
Then read the sentence out loud.

1. I helped Dad _____ the bags from the car.
   unload   unseal

2. I _____ eating cold pizza.
   distrust   dislike

3. Let's _____ the leftover pizza for lunch.
   remove   reheat

4. Chen will _____ the story a second time.
   retell   rewash

5. That water is _____ so don't drink it.
   unload   unclean

6. I _____ with your answer.
   dislike   disagree

Dictation ··

_____

Write It

Focus A suffix is a word part added to the **end** of a word. Each suffix has a meaning. Knowing what a suffix means helps you know what a word means.

ful = full of	**less** = without
color + **ful** = color**ful**	fear + **less** = fear**less**

Add each suffix to the end of the base word.
Write the two new words on the lines. Then read the words you wrote.

base word	ful	less
1. help	_____	_____
2. use	_____	_____
3. power	_____	_____
4. care	_____	_____
5. harm	_____	_____
6. thank	_____	_____
7. pain	_____	_____
8. hope	_____	_____

Dictation ●

1. _____   2. _____   3. _____

Write It

Focus A suffix is a word part added to the **end** of a word. Each suffix has a meaning. Knowing what a suffix means helps you know what a word means.

ful = full of	**less** = without
fear**ful** = full of fear	fear**less** = without fear

Read the definition. Write the correct suffix after the base word. Then write the new word.

1. without care   care_____   _____

2. full of power   power_____   _____

3. full of cheer   cheer_____   _____

4. without fear   fear_____   _____

5. full of color   color_____   _____

6. without pain   pain_____   _____

7. full of peace   peace_____   _____

8. without use   use_____   _____

Dictation ••

_____

Write It

Focus Every suffix has a meaning. Knowing the meaning of a suffix can help you figure out the meaning of a word.

er = someone who
paint + **er** = painter

ly = in a certain way
quiet + **ly** = quietly

Read the base word.
Then write the word using the suffix **er or ly**. The first one is an example.

base word	er	base word	ly
1. play	player	1. quick	_____
2. sing	_____	2. loud	_____
3. work	_____	3. soft	_____
4. teach	_____	4. sad	_____
5. build	_____	5. kind	_____
6. surf	_____	6. near	_____

Dictation ....

_____

Write It

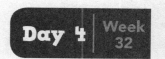

Suffix Box

er   ful   less   ly

One word in each sentence is missing a suffix.
Write the correct suffix to complete the word. Then read the sentence.

1. The farm_____ grows corn.

2. The cat jumped quiet_____ onto the bed.

3. A superhero is power_____.

4. The broken box was use_____.

5. Gramps was cheer_____ when he saw me.

6. The build_____ used bricks to make the house.

7. The nurse spoke kind_____ to me.

Dictation ••

_____

Read It

Write the word that completes the sentence.
Then read the sentence out loud.

1. The snow fell _____ from the black sky.
   softly   sadly

2. I was _____ and I spilled the paint.
   careful   careless

3. The _____ spun around the stage.
   digger   dancer

4. The lion roared _____ at the zebra.
   loudly   smoothly

5. A _____ wind knocked down the oak tree.
   powerless   powerful

6. I'm _____ that you drove me to school.
   thankless   thankful

Dictation ··

_____